HUX 209 Nature and human nature

IMAGINING LANDSCAPES

A portfolio of exhibits

David Wade Chambers

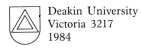
Deakin University
Victoria 3217
1984

Published by Deakin University, Victoria 3217
First published 1982
Revised edition 1985
© Deakin University 1985
Edited and designed by Deakin University
Production Unit
Printed in Hong Kong

National Library of Australia
Cataloguing-in-publication data
Chambers, David Wade, 1938-
    Imagining landscapes

    HUX 209.
    Bibliography.
    ISBN 0 7300 0156 3.
    ISBN 0 7300 0132 6. (HUX 209).

    1. Imagery (Psychology). 2. Nature. I. Deakin
University. School of Humanities. Open Campus
Program. II. Title. III. Title : Nature and human
nature. Portfolio 2.

153.3'2

This book forms part of the HUX 209 *Nature and
human nature*, a course offered by the School of
Humanities in Deakin University's Open Campus
Program. *Imagining landscapes* has been prepared in
collaboration with the course team of HUX 209
Nature and human nature, whose members are:

David Wade Chambers
Max Charlesworth
Lyndsay Farrall (Chairman)
Allan Johnston
Terry Stokes
David Turnbull

The course includes:
Imagining nature (Study guide)
Imagining nature, Portfolio 1: *Putting nature in order*
Imagining nature, Portfolio 2: *Imagining landscapes*
Imagining nature, Portfolio 3: *Is seeing believing?*
Imagining nature, Portfolio 4: *Beasts and other illusions*

Front cover

Fred Williams, *Lightning storm, Waratah Bay*, 1971
Gouache, 59 x 79.5 cm paper size (4 horizontal
images)
National Gallery of Victoria
Presented by the Art Foundation of Victoria with the
assistance of H. J. Heinz II Charitable and Family
Trust, Governor, and the Utah Foundation, Fellow,
1979

Title page

Sir Sidney Nolan, *Wimmera* (from Mount Arapiles),
1943
Ripolin enamel on board, 61 x 91.5 cm
National Gallery of Victoria
Presented by Sir Sidney and Lady Nolan 1983

Georgia O'Keeffe, *Summer days*, 1936 ▶
Oil on canvas, 91.4 x 77.2 cm
Collection Doris Bry, New York, for Georgia O'Keeffe

I have picked flowers where I found them—have
picked up sea shells and rocks and pieces of wood
that I liked ... When I found the beautiful white
bones on the desert I picked them up and took them
home too ... I have used these things to say what is
to me the wideness and wonder of the world as I live
in it ... I was most interested in the holes in the
bones—what I saw through them—particularly the
blue from holding them up in the sun against the
sky ... They were most wonderful against the
Blue—that Blue that will always be there as it is now
after all man's destruction is finished.

Georgia O'Keeffe, 1944

CONTENTS

Ting Yün-p'eng, *The lute song: saying farewell at Hsun-Yang*, c.1575
Hanging scroll, ink and colours on paper, 140.9 x 45.7 cm
Metropolitan Museum of Art, John Stewart Kennedy Fund, 1913

INTRODUCTION

Whether a landscape is seen through the lens of a camera, a telescope, the unaided eye, or even a microscope, the cultural dimensions of that seeing both direct the process and give it meaning.

Clark's discussion may be found in his *Landscape into art,* Harper and Row, New York, 1976.

Three hundred years ago the English word 'landscape' belonged to the painter rather than the topographer. Landscapes were paintings rather than terrain, representations of countryside rather than the countryside itself. Nowadays this emphasis has changed. We think of landscapes as slices of the real world, and the term refers to the physical entity rather than the mental reconstruction.

Yet this slide of meaning, from mode of depiction to the object observed, must not be allowed to hide the fact that the observation of landscape, whether by artist or scientist, geographer or layperson, remains an activity of mind, a mental process through which images of the natural world are formed. Significantly, these images, like those which hang in galleries, often differ profoundly from one culture to another, and, within each culture, from one person to another.

In other words, observers of the same landscape may produce different mental pictures, regardless of their visual acuity or their skill at naturalistic representation. What is actually seen when people look at a natural landscape may vary according to intellectual interests or training, cultural values or expectations, psychological fears or preferences, economic interests, aesthetic sensibilities, and other factors which directly influence the simple act of observation. Thus, what is often taken as an objective process (seeing) necessarily reflects a host of subjective mental operations which together reveal one's personality, social position, culture, and indeed one's humanity. To go a step further, whenever one's perceptions of a natural landscape are recorded for posterity (as in a drawing, painting, map or photograph) matters of artistic and scientific convention additionally influence the resultant image.

Thus, art critic Kenneth Clark's famous contrast of the 'landscape of symbols' with the 'landscape of fact', must not be taken as a hard and fast distinction valid in all historical periods. A landscape painting is rarely purely symbolic and never purely factual. Though it may be approached, the 'landscape of fact', strictly considered, cannot be reached. Because it is ultimately impossible to see and depict nature in its totality and as it really is, devoid of cultural illumination, it may be appropriate to set more attainable goals: realistic and pragmatic standards of naturalistic description.

After all, an individual artist or scientist may well capture and put to use something of the essence and something of the existence (to employ an old philosophical distinction) of any natural object. Yet another generation may see and understand the landscape in an entirely different way. In Clark's discussion of the landscape of fact ('the tame delineation of a given spot', according to the keeper of the Royal Academy), he makes it very clear that facts cannot simply be transposed to canvas: 'facts become art through love, which unifies them and lifts them to a higher plane of reality'. I should like to broaden this notion to include all representation of the natural world. Thus, one might say, facts become art and science through culture, which unifies them and gives them meaning.

1.1
Edward Hopper, *Railroad sunset*, 1929
Oil on canvas, 71.7 x 121.2 cm
Whitney Museum of American Art, New York
Bequest of Josephine N. Hopper

My aim in painting has always been the most exact
transcription possible of my most intimate
impressions of nature. If this end is unattainable, so,
it can be said, is perfection in any other ideal of
painting or in any other of man's activities.

Edward Hopper, 1933

Exhibit 1
IMAGINING THE AMERICAN LANDSCAPE

In 1976 the New York Museum of Modern Art presented an exhibition entitled *The Natural Paradise* which took as one of its major themes the perception of nature in American landscape painting. The following exhibit draws its inspiration from that remarkable bicentennial celebration of the Romantic tradition in American landscape art.

Within that single tradition may be found a great many different ways of seeing and portraying nature, some of which are illustrated in the selection of pictures that follow. They are presented here without comment, but with quotations (usually from the artist) indicating something more about how each thinks about nature and how each works in relation to nature. The procedures below suggest a preliminary way of working through these ideas:

EXERCISE

Consider the meanings of nature and natural discussed in other books in this series. You may wish to propose, and also to criticise, possible criteria for naturalistic description, such as, 'conveys no false information' or 'universally recognised as an accurate portrayal'. This question is treated in greater depth in *Imagining nature* (pp. 27–38) and in *Beasts and other illusions* (pp. 24–42).

1 **Study each of the paintings reproduced. Do not read the accompanying quotations.**

2 **List all those paintings you would describe as 'naturalistic'.**

3 **List any paintings which, though perhaps not fully 'naturalistic', you would describe as 'true to nature' in some more general sense.**

4 **Study again each of the paintings, but this time read the associated quotations. Write down any evidence of visual confirmation of the verbal statement.**

5 **Note and discuss any apparent contradictions between written and pictorial statements.**

6 **Compare and contrast the written quotations without special reference to the associated paintings. Record any broad areas of agreement or general correspondence of approach. Do the same for any divergence of opinion or approach. While definitive discussion of the artistic approach, or opinions, of the artists represented is beyond the scope of this exercise, you should be prepared to make preliminary judgements on these matters based on the information at your disposal.**

7 **Which of these quotations (all made by artists) could as well have been made by scientists about their own work?**

1.2
Maxfield Parrish, *The spirit of transportation*, 1920
Oil on board, 90.2 x 69.9 cm
Clark Equipment Company, Buchanan, Michigan

I feel that the broad effect, the truth of nature's mood attempted, is the most important ... 'Broad effect' is a rather vague term, but what is meant is that those qualities which delight us in nature – the sense of freedom, pure air and light, the magic of distance, and the saturated beauty of colour, must be convincingly stated ... If these abstract qualities are not in a painting it is a flat failure.

Maxfield Parrish, 1935

Numerous modern artists are distinguished by a feeling for nature which has made landscape, instead of mere imitation, a vehicle of great moral impressions.

Henry T. Tuckerman, 1867

1.3
Albert Ryder, *Toilers of the sea*, n.d.
Oil on wood, 29.2 x 30.4 cm
Metropolitan Museum of Art
George A. Hearn Fund, 1915

Ryder gave us first and last an incomparable sense of pattern and austerity of mood. He saw with an all too pitiless and pitiful eye the element of helplessness in things, the complete succucing of things in nature to those elements greater than they that wield a fatal power ... He knew the fine distinction between drama and tragedy, the tragedy which nature prevails upon the sensitive to accept. He was the painter poet of the immanent in things.

Marsden Hartley, 1921

A picture must have a sound structure with all parts coordinated. This inner structure must be the result of the close study of nature's laws, and not of human invention. The artist must come to nature, not with a ready-made formula, but in humble reverence to learn. The work of an artist is superior to the surface appearance of nature, but not its basic laws.

Charles Burchfield, 1945

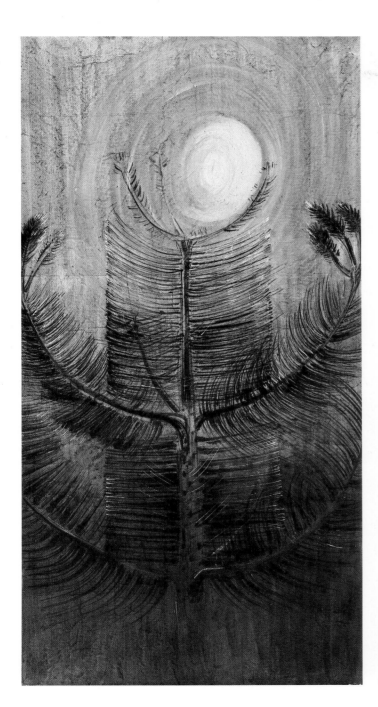

1.4
Morris Graves, *Joyous young pine,* 1944
Watercolour and gouache, 136.2 x 68.6 cm
Collection, Museum of Modern Art, New York
Purchase

I paint to rest from the phenomena of the external
world—to pronounce it—and to make notations of its
essences with which to verify the inner eye.

Morris Graves, 1948

1.5
Andrew Wyeth, *Spring beauty,* 1943
Drybrush and ink, 50.8 x 76.2 cm
F.M. Hall Collection,
Sheldon Memorial Art Gallery
University of Nebraska—Lincoln

I do an awful lot of thinking and dreaming about
things in the past and the future—the timelessness of
the rocks and the hills—all the people who have
existed there. I prefer winter and fall, when you feel
the bone structure in the landscape—the loneliness of
it—the dead feeling of winter. Something waits
beneath it—the whole story doesn't show.

Andrew Wyeth, 1965

1.6
Thomas Moran, *The chasm of the Colorado*, 1873–4
Oil on canvas, 214.4 x 367.7 cm
National Museum of American Art, Smithsonian
Institution
Lent by the U.S. Dept of the Interior, Washington,
D.C.

Mountains are to the rest of the body of the earth,
what violent muscular action is to the body of man.
The muscles and tendons of its anatomy are, in the
mountain, brought out with fierce and convulsive
energy ... But there is this difference between the
action of the earth, and that of a living creature, that
while the exerted limb marks its bones and tendons
through the flesh, the excited earth casts off the flesh
altogether, and its bones come out from beneath.

John Ruskin, 1843

1.7
Augustus Vincent Tack, *Aspiration,* c.1931
Oil on canvas, 194.3 x 344.2 cm
The Phillips Collection, Washington, D.C.

Valley ... walled in by an amphitheatre of
mountains as colossal as to seem an adequate setting
for the Last Judgement, glacial lakes lay like jewels
on the breast of the world—malachite and jade—
greens of every variation. Battlements and pinnacles
of rock close to the clouds and on the mountain
slopes great white glaciers seem motionless and
slumbering, but terrible in their potentialities.

Augustus Vincent Tack, 1920

1.8
Winslow Homer, *Northeaster*, 1895
Oil on canvas, 87.6 x 127.6 cm
Metropolitan Museum of Art, New York
Gift of George A. Hearn, 1910

If you have lived by the sea, you have learned the significance of the bravery of sea people, and you learn to understand and excuse the sharpness of them which is given them from battle with the elemental facts they are confronted with at all times. That is the character of Homer, that is the quality of his painting.

Marsden Hartley, 1921

The best emblem of unwearied, unconquerable power, the wild, various, fantastic, tameless unity of the sea; what shall we compare to this mighty, this universal element, for glory and for beauty? Or how shall we follow its eternal changefulness of feeling? It is like trying to paint a soul.

John Ruskin, 1843

1.9
Marsden Hartley, *Evening storm, Schoodic Maine*, 1942
Oil on composition board, 76.2 x 101.6 cm
Collection, Museum of Modern Art, New York
Acquired through the Lillie P. Bliss Bequest

I have made the complete return to nature, and
nature is, as we all know, primarily an intellectual
idea. I am satisfied that painting also is, like nature,
an intellectual idea, and that the laws of nature as
presented to the mind through the eye—and the eye
is the painter's first and last vehicle—are the means
of transport to the real mode of thought; the only
legitimate source of aesthetic experience for the
intelligent painter . . .

Marsden Hartley, 1928

1.10
Clyfford Still, *1954*, 1954
Oil on canvas, 288.3 x 396.2 cm
Albright-Knox Art Gallery, Buffalo
Gift of Seymour H. Knox, 1957

I'm not interested in illustrating my time ... Our age – it is of science – of mechanism – of power and death. I see no virtue in adding to its mammoth arrogance the compliment of graphic homage.

Clyfford Still, 1963

1.11
Georgia O'Keeffe, *Orange and red streak*, 1919
Oil on canvas, 69.2 x 59.1 cm
Collection Doris Bry, New York, for Georgia
O'Keeffe

I lived on the plains of North Texas for four years
... That was my country—terrible winds and a
wonderful emptiness.

Georgia O'Keeffe, 1970

Another Georgia O'Keeffe landscape and quotation
appears on the contents page.

1.12
Jackson Pollock, *The deep*, 1953
Oil and enamel on canvas, 220.3 x 150.2 cm
Centre National d'Art et de Culture Georges
Pompidou, Musée National d'Art Moderne, Paris
Given in Memory of John de Menil by his children,
the Menil Foundation and Samuel J. Wagstaff, Jr

I am Nature.

Jackson Pollock, 1942

My concern is with the rhythms of nature . . . the
way the ocean moves . . . I work from the inside out,
like nature.

Jackson Pollock, 1955–56

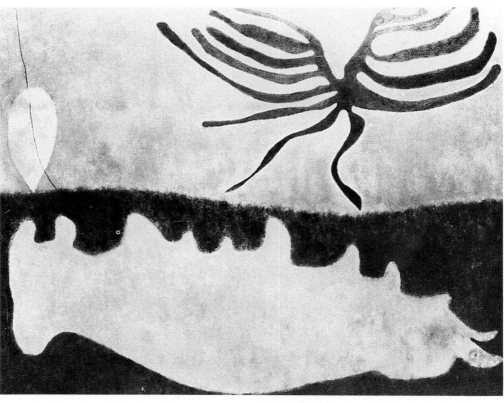

1.13
William Baziotes, *Primeval landscape*, 1953
Oil on canvas, 152.4 x 182.9 cm
Samuel S. Fleisher Art Memorial
Courtesy Philadelphia Museum of Art

Everyone of us finds water either a symbol of peace
or fear. I know I never feel better than when I gaze
for a long time at the bottom of a still pond.

William Baziotes, 1948

1.14
Barnett Newman, *Pagan void*, 1946 ▶
Oil on canvas, 83.8 x 96.6 cm
Collection Annalee Newman, New York

Communion with nature, so strongly advocated by
the theorists as the touchstone of art, the primal
aesthetic root, has almost always been confused with
a love of nature. And the artist falling in love with
the trees and the sea, the beast and the bird, has not
so much been in love with them as with his own
feelings about them . . . The concept of communion
became a *reaction to* rather than a *participation with*,
so that a concern with nature, instead of doing what
it was supposed to do – give man some insight into
himself as an object of nature – accomplished the
opposite and excluded man: setting him apart to
make nature the object of romantic contemplation.

Barnett Newman, 1947

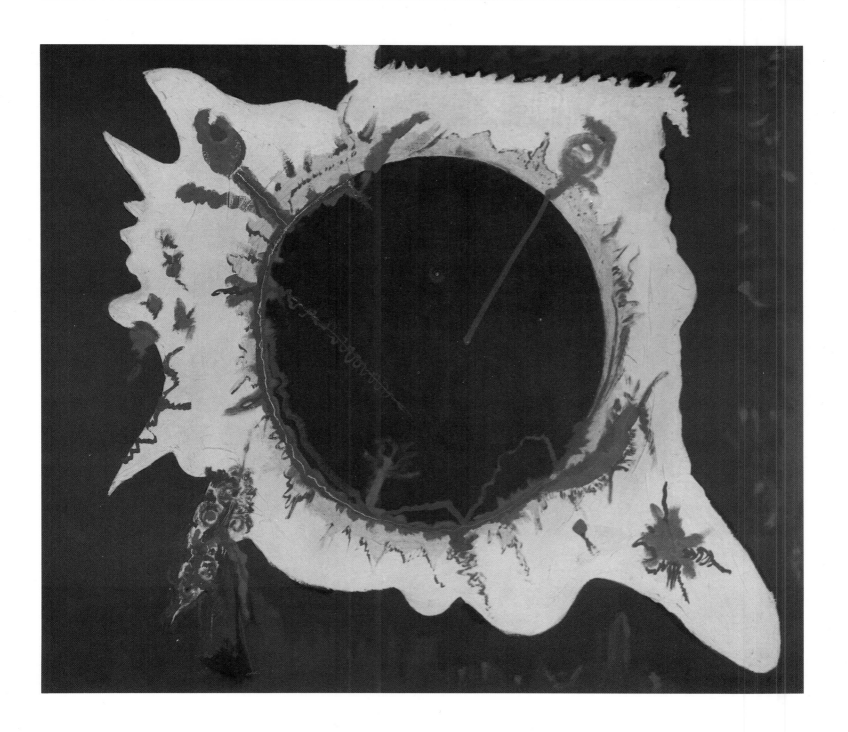

1.15
Theodoros Stamos, *The fallen fig*, 1949
Oil on composition board, 121.9 x 65.7 cm
Museum of Modern Art, New York
Given anonymously

The work of Theodoros Stamos, subtle and sensuous
as it is, reveals an attitude toward nature that is closer
to true communion. His ideographs capture the
moment of totemic affinity with the rock and the
mushroom, the crayfish and the seaweed. He re-
defines the pastoral experience as one of participation
with the inner life of the natural phenomenon. One
might say that instead of going to the rock, he comes
out of it.

Barnett Newman, 1947

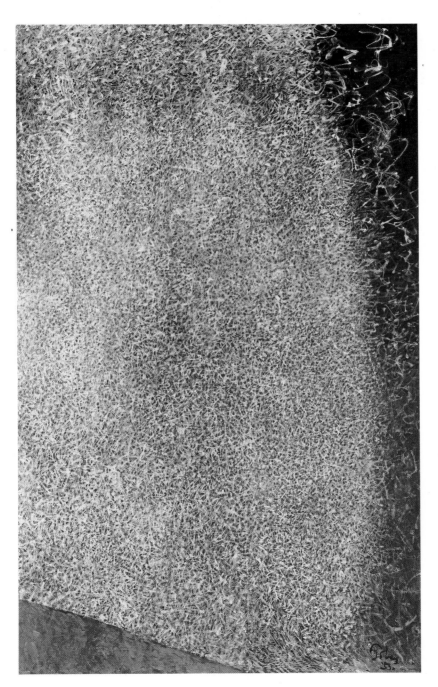

1.16
Mark Tobey, *Edge of August*, 1953
Casein on composition board, 121.9 x 65.7 cm
Collection, Museum of Modern Art, New York
Purchase

Threading light: White lines symbolise light as a
unifying idea which flows through compartmented
units of life, bringing a dynamic to men's minds ever
expanding their energies toward a larger relativity.

Mark Tobey, 1944

My imagination, it would seem, has its own
geography.

Mark Tobey, 1951

1.17
Arthur G. Dove, *Sunrise III*, 1937
Wax emulsion on canvas, 63.2 x 89.2 cm
Yale University Art Gallery
Gift of Katherine S. Dreier to the Collection Société
Anonyme

Why not make things look like nature? Because I do
not consider that important and it is my nature to
make them this way.

Arthur G. Dove, 1927

Maybe the world is a dream and everything in it is
your self.

Arthur G. Dove, n.d.

1.18
John Marin, *Study of the sea*, 1917
Watercolour and charcoal, 40.6 x 48.2 cm
Columbus Gallery of Fine Arts, Columbus, Ohio
Gift of Ferdinand Howald

1.19
John Marin, *Camden Mountain across the bay*, 1922
Watercolour, 43.8 x 52.1 cm
Collection, Museum of Modern Art, New York
Gift of Abby Aldrich Rockefeller (by exchange)

There are certain laws, certain formulae. You have to
know them. They are nature's laws and you have to
follow them just as nature follows them. You find the
laws and you fill them in in your pictures and you
discover that they are the same laws as in the old
pictures. You don't create the formulae . . . You see
them.

John Marin, 1937

Seems to me the true artist must perforce go from
time to time to the elemental big forms—Sky, Sea,
Mountain, Plain—and those things pertaining thereto,
to sort of nature himself up, to recharge the battery.
For these big forms have everything. But to express
these, you have to love these, to be a part of these in
sympathy. One doesn't get very far without this love,
this love to enfold too the relatively little things that
grow on the mountain's back.

John Marin, 1928

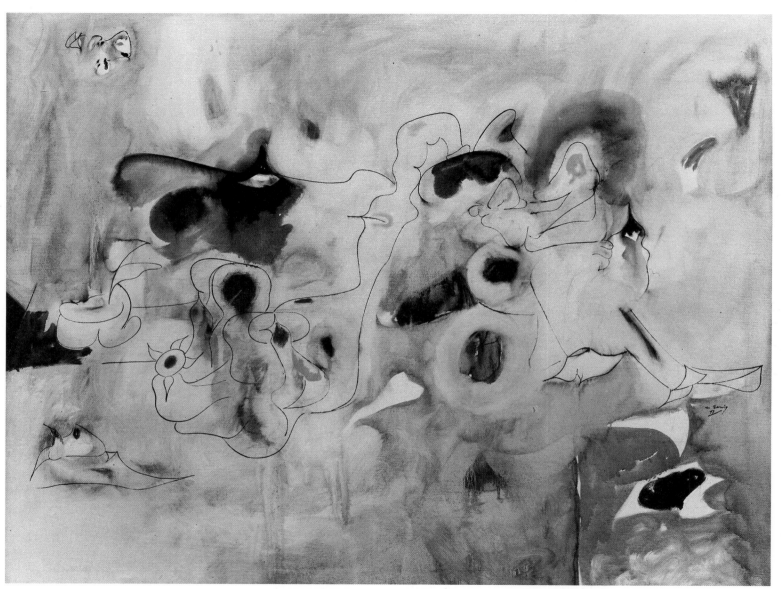

1.20
Arshile Gorky, *The plough and the song,* 1947
Oil on canvas, 128.9 x 159.3 cm
Allen Memorial Art Museum, Oberlin College
R.T. Miller, Jr Fund

The artist cannot avoid nature and his return to it should not be equated with primitivism but instead a re-evaluation of nature based on the new experiences perceived through the complexity of civilization . . . Perceiving nature through the eyes of civilization brings to great art more authority and strength.

I do not paint in front of but from within nature.

Art is a very personal poetic vision or interpretation conditioned by environment.

Arshile Gorky, c.1940–1945

1.21
Arshile Gorky, *Housatonic Falls*, 1942–3
Oil on canvas, 86.3 x 111.76 cm
Reproduced from *Arshile Gorky. The implications of symbols,* by Harry Rand. Allanheld, Osmun & Co, New Jersey, 1981
Location of original unknown

1.22
Anon, *Housatonic Falls*, n.d.
Photograph
The New Milford Historical Society,
New Milford, Connecticut

It is clear just how accurate Gorky's representation is. He showed Housatonic Falls as a low, wide, rocky bench in the river. The falls entirely crossed the stream where it passed through a short but narrow gorge that abruptly rose at that point in the river. Just at that spot the river crashed over the falls and then, constricted by the gorge, flowed on turbulently.

Harry Rand, 1980

FURTHER
READING
Conron, John (ed.), *The American landscape,* Oxford University Press, New York, 1974
McShine, Frank (ed.), *The natural paradise,* Museum of Modern Art, New York, 1976
Novak, Barbara, *Nature and culture,* Oxford University Press, New York, 1982
Stilgoe, John R., *Common landscape of America, 1580 to 1845,* Yale University Press, New Haven, 1982

Exhibit 2
SEEING THROUGH CULTURAL LENSES

ITEMS **2.1** and **2.2** portray precisely the same landscape, the well-known 'Jaws of Borrowdale' at Derwentwater in the English Lake District. The brush and ink drawing (ITEM **2.1**) was painted by a Chinese writer and artist and published in a volume in which he describes his extensive travels through the English countryside. ITEM **2.2** is a lithograph produced a little over one hundred years earlier by an anonymous Englishman. The two pictures were first compared by art historian and theorist E.H. Gombrich, in *Art and illusion*, where he raised a number of interesting issues centring on the question: how much of what we call 'seeing' is conditioned by cultural habits and expectations?

As you compare the two pictures ask yourself which you believe is likely to be the more realistic portrayal of the Jaws of Borrowdale. Which representation, on the other hand, is more heavily laden with cultural convention?

2.1
Chiang Yee, *Cows in Derwentwater*, 1936
Brush and ink
From Chiang Yee, *The silent traveller*, London, 1937

DERWENT WATER,

LOOKING TOWARDS BORROWDALE.

2.2
Anonymous, *Derwentwater, looking toward Borrowdale,*
1826
Lithograph
Crown Copyright Victoria and Albert Museum,
London

Chiang Yee helped us to see the English countryside through Chinese eyes. His painting of the Jaws of Borrowdale follows Chinese stylistic traditions which have endured a thousand years. 'White clouds of mist which like a belt encircle the mountain's waist' may be seen in paintings of the Sung dynasty and earlier. And so also may be found, throughout the intervening centuries, trees with heavily gnarled trunks and exposed roots and leaves of the same tightly controlled brushwork.

2.3
Wen Cheng-Ming, *Seven juniper trees* (detail), 1532
Handscroll, ink on paper: painting only, 28 x 361.9 cm
Honolulu Academy of Arts
Gift of Mrs Carter Galt, 1952

The lute song by Ting Yün-p'eng (opposite page one) further illustrates the Chinese landscape tradition.

2.4
Mi Yu-Jen, *Cloudy mountains* (detail), 1130 A.D.
Sung Dynasty
Handscroll; ink, white lead & traces of colour on silk, 43.4 x 194.3 cm
Cleveland Museum of Art
Purchase from the J.H. Wade Fund

2.5
Shen Chou, *Twelve views of Tiger Hill: Oak and hummocks with three figures at a well*, 15th c.
Ink & slight colour on paper, 31.1 x 40.2 cm
Cleveland Museum of Art
Leonard C. Hanna, Jr, Bequest

2.6
Landscape with piping shepherd and a flight to Egypt,
after Claude Lorraine
Oil on canvas, 103.5 x 135.2 cm
National Gallery of Victoria
Felton Bequest 1946

2.7
George Caleb Bingham, *A view of a lake in the
mountains,* c.1853
Oil on canvas, 53.3 x 79.4 cm
Los Angeles County Museum of Art
Los Angeles County Funds

Though it may not be obvious to European eyes, the anonymous English lithograph (ITEM 2.2) also derives from a distinctive and coherent tradition which, though certainly less ancient and perhaps less rigid than the Chinese, nevertheless comprises a learned vocabulary of technique and convention. These ready formulae, tagged by art historians as ideal, sublime, romantic or picturesque in accord with well developed aesthetic theories of the time, have become for people of European culture a way of looking at the natural world, a way of seeing nature. Thus, when we look at a landscape painting which follows these traditional modes, cultural and stylistic components of the representation are often completely overlooked. For example, we may imagine a picture to be extremely close to nature while in fact it is composed entirely of artistic conventions. Thousands of compositions, including those shown here, portray geographical locations around the world which lend themselves to this treatment.

Conversely, when looking out across a natural landscape, we often choose to focus on those aspects of the view we deem 'picturesque', a word which originally referred to a fit subject for painting (according to the prevailing aesthetic canon) but which has come to mean simply 'pretty as a picture'. The earlier more philosophical use of the term picturesque might include elements considered ugly in themselves, say a gypsy's hovel, harmoniously integrated into the composition, whereas the later more commonplace usage becomes synonymous with 'beautiful'. But it is significant that in either usage the eye has learned to respond to select qualities in nature abstracted from other qualities which are ignored.

Even Chiang Yee, painting for a Western audience, makes some use of the European idiom. His horizontal rectangular frame (ITEM 2.1) for instance, is certainly not of the Chinese tradition. His twin trees in the foreground are decidedly Claudian (i.e. influenced by Claude Lorraine) in placement, though not in technique. Finally, one might even cite the inclusion of cattle as far more common in European than Chinese landscapes. Thus, we see how depictions of nature may be influenced by training, cultural tradition and intended audience.

2.8
Amelia Long (1772–1837), *Landscape with a river,* n.d.
Wash and black chalk on blue paper
Trustees of the British Museum

2.9
Julius Caesar Ibbetson, *A view on Lake Windermere,*
looking towards Ambleside, c.1805
Oil on canvas, 50.1 x 64.2 cm
Yale Center for British Art
Paul Mellon Collection

2.10
E.A. Ife, *A grey evening, Borrowdale*, 1932
Photograph from *The English landscape in picture,
prose and poetry*, by Kathleen Conyngham Greene,
Nicholson and Watson Ltd, London, 1932

Let us return now to the question originally raised in connection with the two pictures (ITEMS **2.1** and **2.2**) of the English Lake District: which is the more realistic portrayal of the Jaws of Borrowdale? Granted that they both make use of aesthetic conventions and compositional formulae, can it be said that one imitates nature more accurately than the other?

After several years of posing this question to 'European' students in America and Australia, I can say that a large number of them assured me with great confidence that the European landscape tradition is more realistic, while the Chinese is more stylised. They felt that Chiang Yee's picture relies more on cultural convention and less on the constraints of topographic reality than does the English picture. More, however, felt unable to decide the issue while a very small number chose the Chinese as a better mirror of reality.

The photographs (ITEMS **2.10** and **2.11**) were taken within a short distance of the same location and within a few years of Chiang Yee's visit. Do they help us resolve the matter? Leaving aside the important fact that a photograph itself is a composed representation of the landscape (and thus may itself be judged a good likeness or a bad likeness), we still face a considerable dilemma. Even standing on the lakeshore with the two paintings in hand, a final judgement on their relative realism would depend on the angle and quality of light, and time of day, season and weather. It might vary according to the choice of where exactly to stand, which tree, if any, to include in the frame of one's looking, and so on through a wide range of factors. In the process of seeing one is forced to make important decisions about what to leave in the frame and what to leave out. And, within the frame, of what to make note.

In other words, in seeing, one is actually composing a picture of reality, a process not unlike that used by each of the two artists. The mental pictures thus constructed will of necessity delete certain small details, perhaps twigs, sedge, a bird, reflections in the water, movement, mist, stones, etc. which, taken together, may be quite significant.

All this is intended simply to confirm that the process of seeing, like the process of representation, is, in its very essence, *selection and interpretation*. But when we compose these mental pictures of reality, what are the criteria, conscious, or more often subconscious, by which we select and interpret?

Exhibit 2 demonstrates some aesthetic and technical factors at work. The exhibits that follow will show additional social, cultural and economic factors which help determine what we actually see when we look at nature.

2.11
E.A. Ife, *Derwentwater*, 1932
Photograph from *The English landscape in picture, prose and poetry*, by Kathleen Conyngham Greene, Nicholson and Watson Ltd, London, 1932

FURTHER
READING

Bicknell, Peter, *Beauty, horror and immensity*, Cambridge University Press, Cambridge, 1981

Clarke, Michael, *The tempting prospect*, Colonade Books, London, 1981

Gombrich, E.W., *Art and illusion*, Princeton University Press, Princeton, 1972 (See especially Chapter 2.)

Hipple, W. J., *The beautiful, the sublime, and the picturesque*, Southern Illinois University Press, Carbondale, 1957

Lee, Sherman, *Chinese landscape painting*, Harper and Row, New York, n.d.

Purkis, John, *The world of the English Romantic poets*, Heinemann, London, 1982

Exhibit 3
COLONIAL
LANDSCAPES

In the second exhibit we studied an example of a Chinese cultural perspective on an English landscape. But what happens when the English travel to other lands? In this exhibit we look at some English views of their own colonial possessions around the globe. Consider first Canada, a country as different from England as can be imagined: a vast country of rugged terrain and harsh light, of brilliant, fiery colours in autumn and of white on white on grey gloom and foreboding in the long winter. Yet if we look at the paintings of colonial Canada, we often find what appears to be a land with a damp, mild climate, planted with familiar (to English eyes) deciduous trees. In most of these pictures one can easily identify the stylistic devices and techniques learned in Europe and transported to the colonies.

3.1
George Heriot, *Chippewa*, 1810 or 1816
Watercolour, 11 x 20 cm
McCord Museum, McGill University, Montreal

George Heriot, like Davies a graduate of Woolwich Military Academy, was a student of the famous English watercolourist Paul Sandby. His style rejects the 'naturalism' of Davies and Sandby, but nevertheless, presents a distinctly British way of seeing Canada. Lord points out that it is a style often associated with the atmospheric views of ruins of the Roman empire, so fondly visited by young British aristocrats of that period. 'Both subjects [Italy and Canada] had to do with empire, since one showed the remains of earlier empires with which the British could compare, while the other indicated how far British rule prevailed.' How far Heriot's work strays from the reality experienced by the Canadian people is indicated by the subject of the painting of Fort Chippewa at a time of intense military activity (war of 1812). 'But this is not what Heriot's imported style had taught him to watch for. Instead, he sees a languid afternoon with a few people out strolling', perfectly suited to his plan to offer for sale views of picturesque Canada (Lord, 1974).

3.2
Thomas Davies, *A view of Montreal in Canada*, 1762
Watercolour, 35.3 x 53.5 cm
National Gallery of Canada, Ottawa

[Davies] has done everything possible to transform
the scene into a picturesque bit of British parkland.
The couple are posed under two trees on the island,
which form an arbour above them. Vines . . . soften
the effect . . . The city of Montreal, just captured by
Davies with British troops two years before, is
rendered accurately enough . . . but we might think
we were along some English riverbank . . . Indeed,
the two natives paddling their canoe along the shore
may very well have been added as an afterthought,
for the express purpose of situating the picture in the
New World.

Barry Lord, 1974

3.3
Thomas Davies, *On the River La Puce*, 1789
Watercolour, 34 x 51.6 cm
National Gallery of Canada, Ottawa

Although trained in the 'objective' techniques of
topographical painting (used for purposes of military
reconnaissance) and although a keen botanist, twenty-
five years later Davies' style, while more vivid and
experimental, still had not come to terms with the
Canadian environment. Here he manages to capture
the rampant growth of Canadian spring, but the
quasi-tropical plant forms and habits of growth are a
complete failure.

3.4
James Edward Hervey MacDonald, *Algoma waterfall,*
(detail), 1920
Oil on canvas, 76.3 x 88.5 cm
The McMichael Canadian Collection
Gift of Col. R.S. McLaughlin

European hegemony in landscape painting was finally replaced in the twentieth century by a distinctively Canadian way of seeing the natural environment. At the very time that a national political identity was being forged, the first national 'school' of painters, the Group of Seven, was formed under the influence of the work of Tom Thomson. These artists challenged the European techniques which failed to capture much of what Canadians value in their landscape.

The birth of a national landscape art in Canada, perhaps paradoxically, meant replacing a 'naturalism', derived from tired European formulae, with a 'realism' that was thought truer to nature in its play of light and colour, mood, movement and form. For someone unfamiliar with the Canadian countryside, the canvasses of the first national 'school', the Group of Seven, might be thought to lean to abstraction, yet for Canadians their great strength is their faithfulness to nature.

3.5
Lawren Stewart Harris, *Eclipse Sound and Bylot Island,* 1930
Oil on panel, 30.2 x 38 cm
The McMichael Canadian Collection
Gift of Col. R.S. McLaughlin

3.6
James Edward Hervey MacDonald, *Autumn, Algoma*,
1920
Oil on pressed board, 21.4 x 26.6 cm
The McMichael Canadian Collection
Gift of Mr R.A. Laidlaw

3.8
John Boyle, *Midnight oil: ode to Tom Thomson*
(detail), 1969
Oil on wood, 243.7 x 248.7 x 83.8 cm
London Regional Art Gallery
General purchase fund
By permission of the artist

3.7
Lawren Stewart Harris, *Montreal River,* 1920
Oil on panel, 26.9 x 34.8 cm
The McMichael Canadian Collection

Compare this with Davies' Montreal river landscape
(ITEM **3.2**).

3.9
Arthur Lismer, *Rain in the north country*, c.1920
Oil on panel, 22.3 x 30.0 x 1.7 cm
The McMichael Canadian Collection
Anonymous donor

3.11
Thomas John (Tom) Thomson, *Windy day*, n.d.
Oil on panel, 21.6 x 26.7 cm
The McMichael Canadian Collection
Gift of Mr R.A. Laidlaw

3.10
Alfred Joseph Casson, *Trees*, 1920
Oil on panel, 24.6 x 28.6 cm
The McMichael Canadian Collection
Gift of Mr H.S. Palmer

3.12
Franklin Carmichael, *La cloche, silhouette*, 1939
Oil on mahogany panel, 25.5 x 30.5 cm
The McMichael Canadian Collection
Anonymous donor

3.13
Arthur Lismer, *Moon River, Georgian Bay,* 1931
Oil on panel, 30.8 x 39.3 cm
The McMichael Canadian Collection
Gift of Mr and Mrs W.J.P. Cannon

Having seen how the Canadian landscape was depicted during the colonial period, we should not be surprised to learn that when Europeans came to depict Australia, a dry country of open everbluegreen forests, utterly unlike either Canada or England, their cultural and artistic training prevailed. Throughout the nineteenth century, romantic and picturesque renderings of the Australian bush abound.

3.14
W. Woolnoth (after W. Westall), *View on the north side of Kangaroo Island,* 1814
Engraving from Flinders, *Voyage to Terra Australis 1801–1803,* London, 1814

3.15
Conrad Martens, *North Head from Balmoral,* 1874
Watercolour, 43.4 x 64.7 cm
Dixson Galleries, Sydney

3.16
Eugene von Guerard, *Mount Kosciusko*, 1866
Oil on canvas, 107 x 153 cm
National Gallery of Victoria
Purchased with the assistance of a Government
Grant 1870

We may accept the abundant evidence that colonial painters often portrayed bushland as parkland, but did they really see it that way? Did they truly believe their pictures gave honest account of what they had seen? Art historian Bernard Smith has assembled a number of verbal descriptions by early explorers and settlers which seem to suggest that many did see with English eyes. Consider, for example the words of artist Sydney Parkinson, naturalist on Cook's first voyage: 'The country looked very pleasant and fertile; and the trees, quite free from underwood, appeared like plantations in a gentlemen's park'. Elizabeth Macarthur wrote in a letter to her friend, a Miss England, 'the greater part of the country is like an English park'.

3.17
Joseph Lycett, *View upon the South Esk River*, 1820
Aquatint, hand-coloured
From *Views in Australia, or New South Wales and Van Diemen's Land delineated*, London, 1824–5.

The greens in the landscape by convict artist Joseph Lycett are those of an English pastureland. The dense forest in the background is really nothing like the open Australian bush, although several trees in the fore and middle ground are recognisably eucalypts and others sustain what might be called a 'rough go' at the casuarina (she-oak). Were it not for the encampment on the river bank, the look of an English country estate would be quite marked. Lycett fails with the casuarina in much the same way that Davies fails with Canadian vegetation on the River Puce (see ITEM **3.3**): certain details are captured but the overall configuration of the tree is lost.

3.18
J.W. Huggins (artist), E. Duncan (engraver), *Swan River 50 miles up*, 1827
Coloured aquatint, 25 x 35.4 cm
Rex Nan Kivell Collection,
National Library of Australia

Whatever his or her artistic training, no observer could long ignore the essential differences of the English and the Australian landscape. After all, the interest of their European audience might be expected to focus precisely on what was novel in these 'new' lands. Thus, artists included within the confines of their noble parks 'exotic' artefacts such as we see in ITEM **3.18**: native people, black swans, grass trees, kangaroos, and in the grove across the river an araucaria (the pine-like tree in the middle).

Before reading on, take a moment to compare the two paintings (ITEMS **3.19** and **3.20**). Can you guess what city is depicted?

Unless you are familiar with either of the pictures, you might be forgiven for naming almost any city of the British empire in the early 19th century. In fact it is not one city, but two. The city in ITEM **3.20** is Hamilton, Ontario (1853) and that in ITEM **3.19** is Sydney, New South Wales (1794), both of course painted according to European aesthetic formulae. Thus, artists went out from the imperial centre to paint the colonies, and whether in Canada or Australia, the United States or New Zealand, they produced very few surprises. Nor should we expect surprises. Not only were artists limited by their training, but perhaps more importantly, if their work was to be taken seriously, if indeed it was to be understood at all, it had to conform to the accepted idiom of the day. This dictum holds true for our own century. In art, in science, in everyday commerce, we work within accepted paradigms, in accord with rules and methods which, in ordinary circumstances, may not be possible to modify.

Thus, if colonial artists gave us what now seem highly stylised and formularised landscapes, it is not simply that they lacked the skill of natural representation. Elements of these paintings may be highly naturalistic. Rather, the specialised techniques (learned through study and discipline), the mental set, the values, the social interests of these artists, and of their audience, required that they produce the paintings that they did, and even required that they see nature in the way that they did. If they did not see what they expected to find, then they looked until they found it. Nietzsche gave us a hint as to how this selection process works:

> Can Nature be subdued to Arts' constraint?
> Her smallest fragment is still infinite!
> And so he paints but what he likes in it.
> What does he like? He likes what he can paint!
>
> Nietzsche, 1895 (translated in Gombrich, 1977)

Some artists made no pretence of producing an 'objective' representation of a scene from any single point of view but were prepared to produce composite landscapes based on several sketches and then reassembled according to the canons of picturesque beauty. Bernard Smith describes how Thomas Watling, a convict and the first professional painter to reach New South Wales, moved from his first wash drawing of Sydney (ITEM **3.21**) to his final canvas (ITEM **3.19**). Obvious changes include the picturesque break in the horizon line, the framing with trees, and the darkening of the foreground.

3.19
Thomas Watling, *A direct north general view of* _____ ,
1794
Oil on panel, 88.2 x 129.5 cm
Dixson Galleries, Sydney

3.21
Thomas Watling, *Taken from the*
West Side of _____ , 1794
Pen and wash, 38.1 x 52 cm
By courtesy of the Trustees, British Museum (Natural
History)

3.20
Robert Whale, *View of* _____ ,1853
Oil, 90.8 x 120.7 cm
National Gallery of Canada, Ottawa

Some Australian Aboriginal artists have chosen to move outside their traditional forms of landscape representation and have utilised a medium and style resembling in many ways those used by European artists. Thus, in the sense in which we have been using the phrase, it is as if Albert Namatjira was able to see his own tribal homeland through European eyes. In ITEM 3.22 not only has he replaced charcoal, ochre, and vegetable dyes for watercolour, but, more significantly, he follows European perspectival formulae of overlapping planes and colour cadences from distinct reds and yellows to purples and, in the furthest distance, misty blue. The 'Europeanness' of this formula may be seen by a comparison with Cameron's painting of the Scottish highlands, ten thousand miles from Central Australia.

A traditional Aboriginal bark painting
Anonymous
Collection, D. W. Chambers
and R. A. Faggetter

3.22
Albert Namatjira, *Towards the James Range*, 1954
Watercolour, 25 x 35 cm
Private collection, Sydney
By permission of Legend Press, Sydney

Though Namatjira's landscapes are sensitively drawn, contributing to our understanding of the land itself, some have said his popularity resulted from the novelty of a tribal artist painting his own country in the European mode. Yet no European could have produced the landscapes he gave us. His mastery of certain 'naturalistic' techniques and his close knowledge of the land itself are demonstrated in ITEM **3.22** . Consider the remarkable feeling of three dimensions, missing in the Cameron. Consider also which of the paintings would serve as the better 'map' for a person setting out to cross the ranges depicted. Namatjira delineates a landscape, based on close and friendly knowledge. One feels he has seen the other side of each ridge and knows what lies beyond.

3.23
Sir David Young Cameron, *The wilds of Assynt,*
c.1936
Oil on canvas
Collection of Perth Museum and Art Gallery,
Scotland

One of the first artists in Australia to forsake European canons of picturesque beauty was the Englishman John Glover who arrived in Tasmania in 1831 at the age of 64. His intense admiration for Claude may be seen in his portrayal of the English Lake District (ITEM **3.24**) which should be compared with ITEMS **2.2** and **2.6 - 2.11**. As would be expected, a number of his first colonial landscapes followed European formulae. Consider, for example, the 'sublime' vision of ITEM **3.25**, exemplified particularly in the majestic mountain scenery. Then too the rainbow sanctifies and adds mystery to the gloomy precincts of the orphanage. Yet, already his gum trees have a certain credibility as Australian bush, rather than European forest. *The River Nile* (ITEM **3.26**) is one of several canvasses to give us the sensuous Tasmanian bush in true visual independence from the classical patterns of European aesthetic dogma.

3.24
John Glover, *Ullswater*, 1840
Oil on canvas, 76.4 x 114.6 cm
National Gallery of Victoria
Presented by Miss B Hunter, 1840

3.25
John Glover, *Mount Wellington with the Orphan Asylum – Van Diemen's Land*, 1837
Oil on canvas, 76.5 x 114.2 cm
National Gallery of Victoria
Funds provided by the Joe White Foundation, 1981

3.26
John Glover, *The River Nile, Van Diemen's Land,*
c.1838
Oil on canvas, 76.2 x 114.3 cm
National Gallery of Victoria
Felton Bequest 1946

Australian sky and nature awaits, and merits real artists to portray it . . . there is a whole system of landscape painting of the most striking character, yet available for human art . . .

John Lhotsky, 1839

When Claudian approaches to the Australian landscape were finally left behind, it was surely because Australians had ceased to see their land according to 'picturesque' formulae. It probably never seemed 'sublime' to early Australians despite the brilliance of von Guerard's attempt to describe it so (see ITEM **3.16**). However other European movements, for example impressionism and surrealism, showed themselves better adapted to delineate the sear beauty of the Australian bush and the 'savage and scarlet' spirit of its deserts. And in recent years distinctive and sympathetic ways of seeing and depicting Australian sky and nature have begun to emerge. Yet no one style will have all the answers. In each new generation nature must await the appearance of Lhotsky's 'real artists'.

3.27
Hans Heysen, *Sunshine and shadow,* c.1904–5
Oil on canvas, 176.5 x 114.3 cm
National Gallery of Victoria
Felton Bequest, 1906

Further examples of modern Australian landscapes may be found on the cover, title page and in Exhibits Four and Five.

3.28
Frederick McCubbin, *The lost child*, 1886
Oil on canvas, 114.3 x 72.4 cm
National Gallery of Victoria
Felton Bequest, 1940

3.29
Clifton Pugh, *Day of winter,* 1959
Oil on composition board, 68.6 x 91.4 cm
National Gallery of Victoria
Purchased 1959

3.30
Margaret Preston, *Bush track*, 1945
Coloured monotype, 30.5 x 40.5 cm
National Gallery of Victoria
Purchased 1948

3.31
Sydney Nolan, *Central Australia*, 1949
Oil on hardboard, 91.5 x 122 cm
National Gallery of Victoria
Purchased 1950

3.32
Fred Williams, *Wild Dog Creek I*, 1981
Lithograph, 37 x 50 cm
Collection of Deakin University, Geelong

3.33
Fred Williams, *Wild Dog Creek*, 1977
Oil on canvas, 183 x 152.5 cm
Private collection, Melbourne

3.34
Fred Williams, *Kosciusko*, 1975
Gouache, 57 x 76.5 cm
National Gallery of Victoria
Presented by The Art Foundation of Victoria with
the assistance of H. J. Heinz II
Charitable and Family Trust, Governor, and the
Utah Foundation, Fellow, 1979

FURTHER
READING

Carmichael, D. G., *Catalogue of the McMichael Canadian Collection*, Kleinburg, Ontario
Lord, Barry, *The history of painting in Canada*, NC Press, Toronto, 1974
Seddon, G. and Davis, M. (eds), *Man and landscape in Australia*, Australian Government
    Publishing Service, 1976
Smith, Bernard, *European vision and the South Pacific*, Oxford University Press, London,
    1960
Thomas, Daniel, *Outlines of Australian art*, Macmillan, Melbourne, 1973

Exhibit 4
ORDER
AND CHAOS
IN THE
AUSTRALIAN
ENVIRONMENT

What can we know of the Australian environment before European settlement wrought such great changes? While painting and photography are by no means infallible guides to nature as it was, or as it is, we can learn from both. And of course we can learn also from the historical and anthropological records that remain. However, any effort to uncover the authentic early Australian landscape presents us with two very different (indeed in some ways entirely opposed) cultural viewpoints: that of black Australians and that of white Australians. The Aboriginal perspective is that of a profoundly spiritual and yet intensely practical people, living close to the land. Their distinctive culture has excited interest around the world. The European perspective, on the other hand, is that of a displaced people, largely alienated from the land. Their derivative culture provided them with a powerful technology which has seemingly enabled combative triumph over the land and over the people who first inhabited it. Whereas the indigenous Australian perspective evolved over tens of thousands of years, the European–Australian perspective has developed over only two hundred years, applying attitudes to nature which were honed and refined on the other side of the planet.

4.1
Arthur Streeton, *Still glides the stream*, 1890
Oil on canvas, 82.5 x 153 cm
Art Gallery of New South Wales, Sydney

This Yarra River landscape, almost certainly the very view over which Streeton's axeman gazes, is now covered with suburban Melbourne bungalows for ten to twenty miles in every direction.

4.3
Narritjin Maymuru, *Djarrakpi landscape*, c.1978
Traditional bark painting
Reproduced by courtesy of Film Australia, owner of
the painting, and the Aboriginal Artists Agency on
behalf of the Manggalili clan.

This painting depicts both the topographical features
of a particular site and the mythological events which
shaped them.

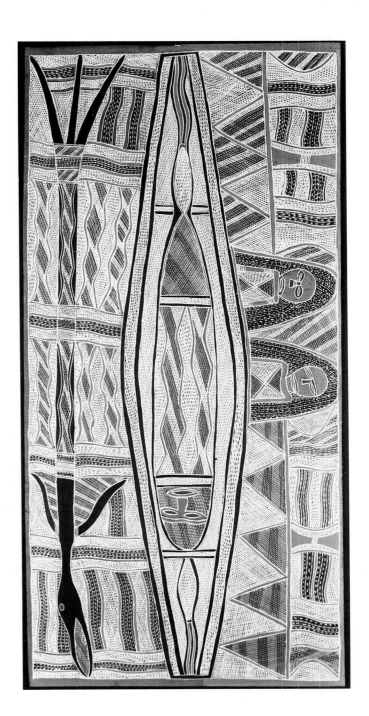

4.2
Arthur Streeton, *The selector's hut: Whelan on the log*, 1890
Oil on canvas, 76.7 x 51.2 cm
Collection Australian National Gallery, Canberra

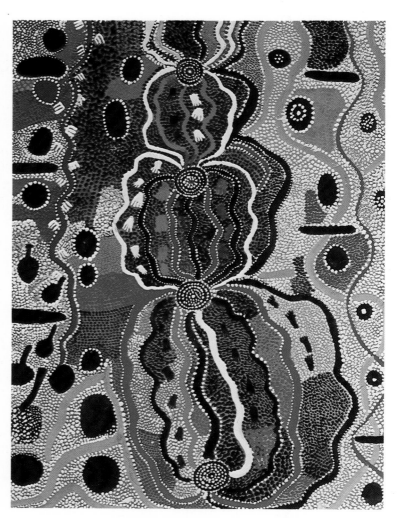

4.4
Johnny Warrangula Tjaparula, *Water dreaming*, 1977
45 x 62 cm
Custodian: Tjaparula-Tjakamara
By permission of Mr Geoff Bardon

4.5
Old Mick Tjakamara, *Children's water dreaming
with possum story*, 1973
45 x 58 cm
Custodian: Old Mick as custodian for his father,
Old Dan Bugger Tjaparula
By permission of Mr Geoff Bardon

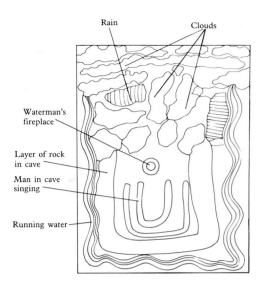

Rain

Clouds

Waterman's fireplace

Layer of rock in cave

Man in cave singing

Running water

Map of the landscape depicted in ITEM **4.4**

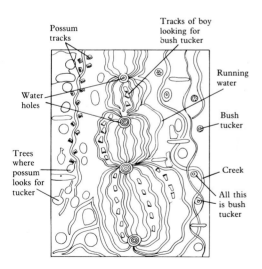

Possum tracks

Tracks of boy looking for bush tucker

Water holes

Running water

Bush tucker

Trees where possum looks for tucker

Creek

All this is bush tucker

Map of the landscape depicted in ITEM **4.5**

To pursue this cultural comparison of human/landscape relations in Australia, we must first attempt to see the landscape through the eyes of its indigenous people — a task in which we can have only the most limited success. Anthropologists tell us that the Aboriginal people discuss the land primarily in terms of its natural products for use in daily life, in terms of their activities and the mythic activities of their ancestors, and in terms of seasonal change. The land is conceived of and understood not only ecologically but mythologically or perhaps better said, religiously.

Aboriginal artists present this vision of the landscape at several levels of reality. Many Aboriginal landscapes are at one level a map of a real landscape, at another level a simple and decorative depiction of objects and creatures in that landscape and, at a third level, a telling of a sacred myth.

> Paintings are important to clan members in two main ways: they establish links between living clan members and the world of the Ancestral Beings who created it, and they are seen as a charter to the land. The intricate background patterns are the unique property of individual clans and are often said to provide the clan with its 'permission' from the Ancestral World to occupy their land ... The paintings represent a way of looking at the world and of ordering life's experiences in terms of the relationship between man and the environment ...
> Each place depicted in the paintings is associated with a set of mythological events which underline the landscape and endow it with meaningful form. The paintings are said to show people the way by revealing the ancestrally determined order of the world. There is a right way and a wrong way to learn and use knowledge.
> Howard Morphy, Manggalili Art: Catalogue, 1983

Every feature of a given landscape may be endowed with meaning. The paths of the Ancestral Beings became rivers and lakes and their bodies were transformed into rocks and trees. A line of rocks at the beach near the mouth of a river may be a manifestation of one of these Ancestral Beings. Thus, much of Aboriginal art is concerned with defining the relationship between objects in the cultural and natural environments. The revelation of new 'meanings' for elements of the art does not negate the old, but adds further to the individual's perception of the multiple and complex relationships existing in the natural world.

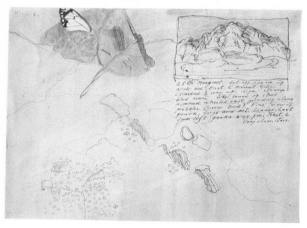

4.6
John Wolseley, *Description of a journey from Ormiston Pound to an ochre mine in the Heavitree Range, Northern Territory* (detail), 1979
Watercolour, each sheet 23.5 x 31.5 cm, overall (inc. frame) 86.2 x 236.2 cm
Geelong Art Gallery
Purchased 1979 Capital Permanent Award

The other ten panels of *Journey from Ormiston Pound* are found on pp. 69–71.

An English Australian artist John Wolseley has commented on the influence of Aboriginal perspectives on his own work.

It is interesting how much we take for granted our own visual symbols. Many of us think that the ubiquitous gum tree and 'view' found in so many Australian lounges is a wonderfully true expression of reality. Whereas it is in fact just one—and often a debased, badly reproduced and trite one at that—of a great variety of models of reality.

I was recently in a house in Alice Springs where there was one of those gum tree reproductions hanging near an acrylic painting of a *Yam Spirit Dreaming* by Tim Leurah Tjapaltjari, similar to one by the same artist illustrated in Geoff Bardon's *Aboriginal Art of the Western Desert*. I decided one way of analysing the nature of the extraordinary difference between the two paintings was to examine how the 'Western' painting as compared to the Aboriginal one was the product of a compartmentalised way of life. The 'isolation' of different elements was apparent all the way from the initial perception of the objects described through to their expression and finally in their significance as finished products.

In the case of the Yam dreaming painting the 'perception' of that plant had come through a lifetime of experiencing it. Not as something out there, but as haptic experience through finding/gathering/eating and also through song cycles and ceremony, the performance of myths about it.

And so when it came to the expression of that plant in the painting several levels of meaning flowed into each other. A 'Western' picture of the same subject would probably not have included the roots—the flowering part would have been cut off and isolated in a pretty vase. The Tjapaltjari painting described the tubers and stems of the plant, and showed how it flowed out into root systems deep in the ground; and then out to the woman searching for the yams, describing with a dark stippling how the grass had been burnt away in the search; and then beyond them to the children playing, watched by birds, dogs and kangaroos. In ways difficult for us to understand that yam dreaming was part of the person who painted it. And yet it also flowed out of him as a totemic expression of the collective unconscious of an ancient culture.

When such an image takes the form of a giant ritual painting on sand (as opposed to this Western-inspired acrylic version on board) its importance is over when the ceremony has been completed, and then it is left behind to be smudged by the feet of geckos and blown away on the desert winds. That seems to me to be the most symptomatic illustration of the difference between the two attitudes to art. The ultimate dislocation! For the urban art product will probably end up as a separate entity on a strangers' wall, appreciated in terms of its relationship to the colour of the curtains or as a totemic expression of its financial value.

(Wolseley, in Carmichael et al., *Orienteering*, DUP, 1983, pp. 141–143)

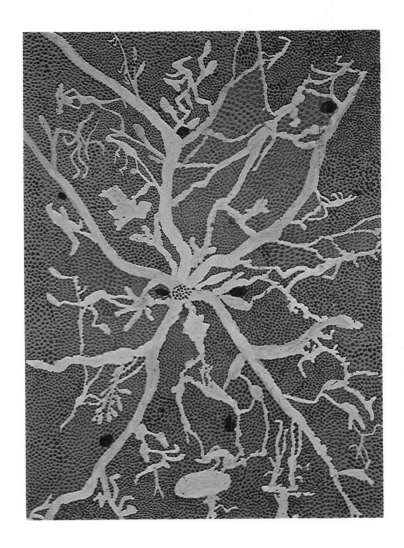

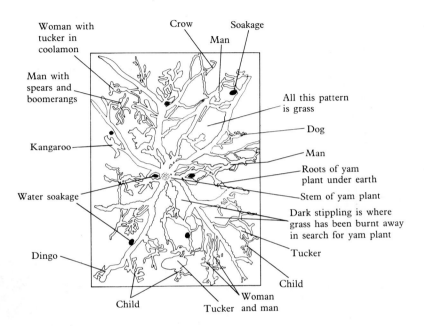

Map of the landscape depicted in ITEM **4.7**

4.7
Tim Leurah Tjapaltjari, *Yam spirit dreaming*, 1972
54 x 70 cm
Custodian: The artist's father Barney Turner
Tjungarrayi
By permission of Mr Geoff Bardon

The painting portrays the ecological associations of
the yam plant and includes figures representing
kangaroo, lizard, dingo, crow, men, women and
children, all connected by the roots of the yam plant
and depicted against a background of grass (dark
stippling), burned grass (red stippling), and marsh
(large dark spots).

In the third exhibit we learned how the first Europeans in Australia saw the land through the cultural and socio-economic lenses of their European experience. Soon after the first heady months of settlement turned into years, letters sent home to England speak less of noble park-like landscapes and more of bleak and gloomy wilderness, infertile soil, low rainfall, deadly snakes, and unfriendly natives. The natives were believed to be of the stone-age, and child-like, with no knowledge whatever worth acquiring. Clearly the land seemed a chaotic and hostile wilderness upon which civilised man would have to impose order, value and meaning.

This view could not be in greater contrast with that of the original inhabitants for whom every feature of the land was already charged with meaning according to a precise order established in the dreamtime and confirmed in daily interaction with the natural environment.

4.8
Joseph Lycett, *Fishing by torchlight*, c.1819
Watercolour, 17.5 x 28 cm
National Library of Australia

Perhaps no more dramatic contrast between the two cultural perspectives on nature can be found than in the reaction to bushfire. Australia is perhaps the most fire-prone of all continents. In the European-Australian painting (ITEM **4.9**) fire is a terrifying menace, unnatural, a hell, a chaos, disorder and destruction. In the Aboriginal view (ITEM **4.10**) below, fire forms part of a gentle peaceful scene, not threatening, but within the order of nature. Of course, fires in nature do in fact range from the holocaust to the 'cool burn', but the attitudes described here are those each culture generalises.

Little did the early settlers know, and indeed only recently have ecologists begun to suggest, that the open woodlands, free of underbrush, which the first colonists described as gentlemen's parks, had resulted from Aboriginal husbandry of the land. Through regular and controlled firing of the land, Aboriginals had established fire breaks early in the dry season, and thus rejuvenated the growing cycle of the natural flora. This was by no means indiscriminate burning: certain plants and human habitations were protected. Wherever the Aboriginal people did not live, or had been driven off or killed, or had died of imported disease, it has been suggested that the woodlands tended to grow a dense understory, providing kindling for calamitous fires, such as those experienced in

4.9
Sir John Longstaff, *Gippsland, Sunday night*, 1898
Oil on canvas, 196.2 x 143.5 cm
National Gallery of Victoria
Purchased 1898

Gippsland (1898) and most recently throughout Victoria and South Australia on Ash Wednesday, 1983. However the ecology of fire in Australia is still a matter for debate. When the anthropologist Rhys Jones once asked some Aboriginals why they burned the land, they responded: 'More better, we clean this country'.

4.10
Dick Roughsey, *Bushfire approaching*, n.d.
Acrylic, 40 x 50 cm
Private collection

4.11
Survey map, township of Airey's Inlet, Victoria
Based on a map provided by the Barrabool Shire
Council, 27.6.73

The order which Europeans imposed on the land was
a geometric grid, bearing little relationship to the
natural features or the ecological realities. The sub-
divisions of Airey's Inlet, though considered by its
inhabitants a 'bush retreat', reflect the shire engineer's
T-square and drawing board rather than the flood
plain of the river, the steep slopes of the Otway
foothills, or the dunes and cliffs of the shores of Bass
Strait.

Fences formed both the physical and symbolic structure of the European conception of
order. Fences imposed on the landscape a new kind of distinction relating to individual
ownership; that is to say, they defined and enforced the concept of property, a legal and
economic notion, unrelated to nature except perhaps in some distant sense to animal
territoriality. In early Australia, fences did not so much divide one neighbour from
another as to draw a line between wilderness and civilisation, between the wild and the
tame, between nature and culture.

4.12
Anon, *The surveyor*, 1876
Engraving

Hidden in the dense Gippsland rain-forest stands a
potent symbol of the reordering of the natural
environment. Today the few remaining pockets of this
forest are threatened by the economic interests of the
new order.

4.13
C.G.S. Hirst, *Claremont House*, 1881
Pen, ink and watercolour, 54.5 x 89 cm
National Library of Australia
(Claremont House is the residence of Mr George
Bashford and family at Limestone, near Ipswich,
Queensland)

4.14
Joseph Lycett, *Raby. A farm belonging to Alexander
Riley Esqr. New South Wales*, c.1824–5
Aquatint
From Joseph Lycett, *Views in Australia or New South
Wales and Van Diemen's Land delineated*, London,
1824–5

4.15
Dinny Nolan, *Water dreaming mythology*, n.d.
Acrylic on canvas, 102 x 152 cm
Collection of Clifton Pugh

The painting of Mikantji, that's my country, not anybody's at all, that's our country. It's our grandfathers' country, fathers' country and we. All the Tjangala and Jampitjimpa are looking after that country.

Dinny Nolan

The concept of property was clearly known to Aboriginal Australians, but defined by sacred sites, by walking tracks, waterholes and bush tucker, and by traditional 'extended family' occupation, rather than by fenced boundaries. Invading Europeans found it difficult to comprehend this concept of property, and, in any case, found it in their interest to disregard it. Aboriginals often speak of their responsibility for protecting and caretaking the land. This aspect of 'property ownership', while very familiar in Europe, was not widespread among the pastoralists and agriculturalists who settled in the colonies. The concept of ownership which prevailed was one which emphasised dominion and rights of exploitation according to private economic interest.

It requires only a slight effort of the mind to see this landscape through the proud eyes of the farmer and an equally slight effort to see it through bewildered Aboriginal eyes.

> The felling or ring-barking of forests, the choking of streams, the destruction of the topsoil—these were mostly the handiwork of agriculturalists; and much of this damage was done after Colonial Australia had gone. Streams, waterholes, lagoons and forests that eighty years of pastoralism had left intact, thirty years of agriculture could and did turn into the sunburnt country.

> Denholm, 1979

This painting may give some impression of the landscape which the Aboriginals see when they say 'This country bin losin' song, eh?' (from a lecture by Rhys Jones, 1981). A geometric order of straight lines and right angles is an abstract and highly arbitrary rearrangement of nature, which to Aboriginal eyes, accustomed to another kind of order, must have appeared as much a chaos and wilderness as the primeval forest seemed to early settlers.

FURTHER READING

Bardon, Geoff, *Aboriginal art of the Western Desert*, Rigby, Adelaide, 1979
Carmichael, Makin and Wolseley, *Orienteering*, DUP, Geelong, 1982
Denholm, David, *The colonial Australians*, Allen Lane, Ringwood, 1979
Flower, Cedric, *The Antipodes observed*, Macmillan, Melbourne, 1975
McCullough, Bianca, *Each man's wilderness*, Rigby, Adelaide, 1980
Morphy, Howard, *Manggalili art: catalogue*, reprint Deakin University, 1983
Powell, J.M., *Environmental management in Australia, 1788–1914*, Oxford University Press, Melbourne, 1980
Powell, J.M. (ed.), *The making of rural Australia*, Sorrett Publishing, Melbourne, 1980
Tuan, Yi-Fu, *Topophilia*, Prentice-Hall, Englewood Cliffs, 1974

4.16
Arthur Boyd, *Berwick landscape*, 1948
Tempera on board, 69.8 x 87.6 cm
Collection of the Queensland Art Gallery

Exhibit 5
IMAGING THE FUTURE LANDSCAPE

The spirit of progress captured in ITEMS **5.1** and **5.3** might be said to glorify ruthless exploitation, unprincipled development and unbridled growth, though clearly the artists foresaw none of this. In America, progress was part of the country's sense of 'manifest destiny' and optimism. Such naivety was in some cases self-defeating, as in the Oklahoma and Texas 'dust bowl', which resulted from 'tractoring out' (as it was said) the grasslands. The principal economic and human cost however, has been measured in environmental pollution, human health, and loss of wildlife and wilderness.

This tide of 'progress' has now been slowed only in the sense that some small pockets of land around the globe have received some protection. But the despoilation of the landscape in which we live continues apace. Each generation sacrifices a proportion of what remains to its short-run economic advantage. The challenge of containing economic development within the constraints of ecological balance has almost nowhere been taken up.

5.1
American progress, 1873
Lithograph after a painting by John Gast
Library of Congress, Washington, D.C.

5.2
Anon, *Making a clearing near Lake Beauport, Lower Canada,* c.1835–6
Watercolour, 14.6 x 23.5 cm
Public Archives of Canada

5.3
Asher B. Durand, *Progress,* 1853
Oil on canvas, 121.9 x 182.8 cm
The Warner Collection of Gulf States Paper
Corporation, Tuscaloasa, Alabama

Smokestacks, a train on a trestle, buildings and
agriculture in the far distance symbolise the
irresistible march of 'progress' and its effects on the
countryside. The watchful Indians from their vantage
point in the natural landscape witness the fall of
Nature and the rise of white man's civilisation. As
historian Leo Marx has pointed out, this canvas
reverses, in a curious way, those romantic nineteenth
century images of the philosopher meditating upon
the ruins of civilisation and the final triumph of
Nature.

5.4
Anon, *Moving day,* c.1875
Photograph

Another vision of the future landscape comes to us from the great landscape gardeners of the eighteenth century: replacing wilderness with paradise. The family which Wheatley painted was not relaxing in a wilderness setting, but rather in a garden, a part of the 'built' environment. In these great parks, we find trees, boulders, lakes and picturesque cottages moved about as if on an artist's palette. Huge drainage channels were installed below and deer above.

Architects, gardeners, planners, and even occasional government officials have been tantalised by the notion of 'garden cities', residential and even industrial precincts reconstructed in a 'natural' setting. Such a notion may or may not be practical, may or may not be desirable; the question we raise here, to which there is no easy answer, is 'are they natural?'

5.5
Francis Wheatley, *George and Mary Browne with their five elder children,* c.1779
Oil on canvas, 75 x 88.9 cm
Yale Center for British Art
Paul Mellon Collection

5.6
Henry Gritten, *Melbourne from the Botanical Gardens,*
1867
Oil on mill board, 29.4 x 44.1 cm
La Trobe Collection, State Library of Victoria

Another approach to the future landscape, arising in part out of the conservation movement, places great value on the preservation of remaining wilderness areas and would restrict or prevent new development of certain environments. Furthermore, it calls, wherever possible, for urban and agricultural development in which native flora and fauna can survive. Preservation of the natural ecology requires a smaller capital investment than the construction and artificial maintenance of exotic parks, such as envisaged by the 'garden' ideal, but, on the other hand, in some cases requires substantial short-term disadvantage to some mining, agricultural and real estate interests.

In this exhibit we have imagined three possible landscapes of future development. The first, unlimited and unrestricted growth, surely spells disaster perhaps even in the short run. The second, recreating the city, as one might say, in God's image, as a garden, seems economically impractical except in certain limited urban situations. The third, an integration of humane ecological values and those of private economic interests, moderates the greed of the first approach and the utopian quality of the second.

5.7
Edward Roper, *Prairie flowers near Broadview, Assiniboia,* 1887
Watercolour on pencil, 51.7 x 31.4 cm
Public Archives of Canada

5.8
Charles McCubbin, *Airey's Inlet,* n.d.
Watercolour, 48 x 30 cm
Collection of the artist

In examining these three possible future landscapes, we are in fact focusing on the influence of cultural factors in the depiction of natural appearance, but the distinction between appearances and their representation in art or science is not, as it might be assumed, a distinction between nature and culture. Seeing and depicting nature are both subject to the dictates of culture. Perception and representation are bounded by the constraints of habit and convention and filtered by networks of expectation, interest and preference.

This realisation, it should be stressed, does not necessarily lead one to an ultimate relativism which refuses to recognise the application of *any* standards of fidelity and truth in the processes of perception and representation. The Renaissance discoveries of the geometry of visual perception are relevant and valuable, if not ultimately reliable, as are the increasingly sophisticated cross-cultural studies of the psychology of perception. While standards based on these and other theoretical assumptions retain certain arbitrary and conventional dimensions, they may still usefully guide our actions in the pursuit of particular goals.

Over a century ago, the painter John Constable compared the art of seeing nature with the art of reading Egyptian hieroglyphs: both are complex skills to be learned. Furthermore, it is not merely the 'mastery of appearance' that must be acquired. Both art and science probe a realism that lies beyond mere appearance and pictorial fidelity.

John Wolesley, detail from *Journey from Ormiston Pound*
(see ITEM **4.6**, p. 54)

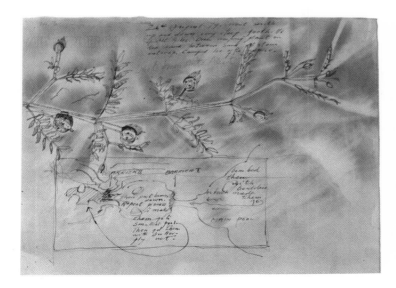

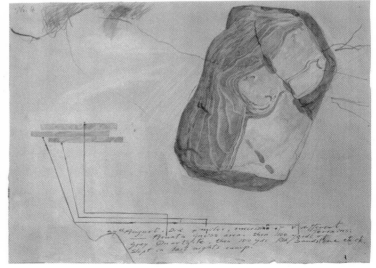

For example, John Wolesley's paintings of Central Australia integrate visual and cognitive truths which, though they do not make up a single perceptual pattern meeting the individual eye, nevertheless provide a richly complex depiction of the defining characteristics of a given landscape. To the extent his vision is accurate he gives us a closer approximation of nature than could ever be achieved by photographic likeness.

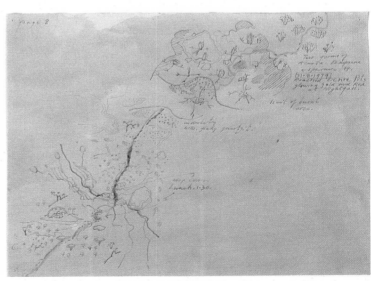

These panels from Wolesley's *Journey from Ormiston Pound* exhibit topographical, geological, botanical, anatomical, historical and aesthetic information as recorded and integrated by the artist during his safari across an Australian desert.

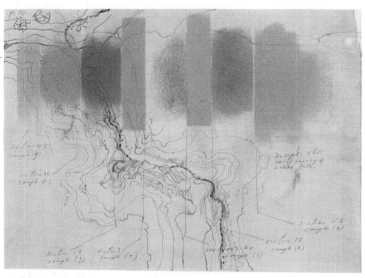

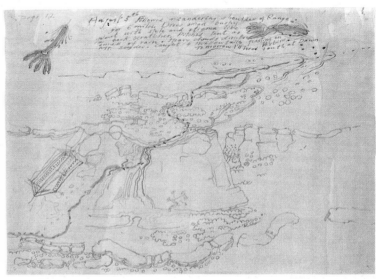

Most importantly, we must remember that there is a close, abiding and interactive relationship between how one sees an environment and how one inhabits, manipulates and influences that environment. A relativism which simply equates the validity of all representations of nature (saying that one picture is as good as any other) precludes the possibility of evaluating or criticising human action.

Through time and across cultures certain modes of representation have enhanced our understanding of humanity's environment and of human interactions with that environment. If one views the Australian environment, for example, with Claudian eyes, impressionist eyes, Aboriginal eyes or with the eyes of a mining engineer, one learns things of value which affect the nature and quality of future environmental encounters.

5.9
Sidney Nolan, *Desert storm,* 1966
Oil on hardboard, seven panels each
152.3 x 122 cm
Collection of the Art Gallery of Western Australia

Panel 1

Panel 2

Seeing Australia's landscape in the way Sidney Nolan sees the Kimberleys is perhaps to forsake once and for all the naive visions of those who destroyed the Victorian mallee lands to grow wheat or of those who converted the Ord River Valley to provide cotton fodder for insects. Any attempt to see the land 'as it is' incorporates an implicit view of the land 'as it will be'. The relationship between seeing and doing, between picturing and interacting, can be surprisingly immediate. Thus, sophisticated analysis of this relationship should be the aim of all who seek to know and work with nature.

Panel 3

Panel 4

Panel 5

Panel 6

Panel 7

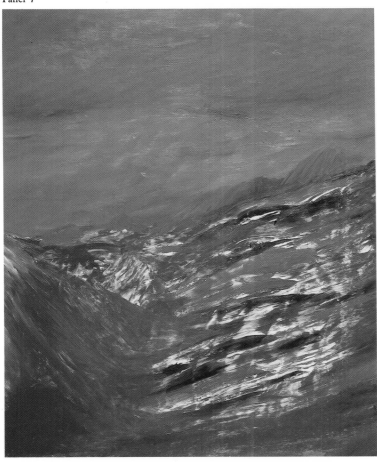

The theme of *Desert Storm* is space and light — and a sudden suffocating, red dark. The seductive blue of an endless distance draws us on ... This blue space is threatened by the dust-storm which blows up ... (in the last three panels). The idyllic desert, beautiful even when it is baleful, can become an inferno of grit.

... *Desert Storm says* what it *is*. The eye was for the Medievals the noblest of the senses, because the most disinterested; and so it was the best image of the spirit. The eye expands through four panels of this vast painting. In three of the panels it is thwarted. The translucid becomes opaque. Stone, ribbed and sharp, asserts touch; the unseen eye-beam is blocked by rock and dust, as the dark, the opaque, the body, and the circumstances of life, block and thwart the soul. Spirit delights in transparency: touch must respond to the hard and the gritty. Touch is not disinterested, it is the very symptom of being in the world, and of boundedness.

P.A.E. Hutchings, Edinburgh 1969, catalogue introduction, *Sydney Nolan: Recent Paintings*, Skinner Galleries, Perth, February 1970

FURTHER READING

Arnheim, R., *Visual thinking*, Faber and Faber, London, 1970

Barlow, E., *Frederick Law Olmsted's New York*, Praeger, New York, 1972

Bazarov, K., *Landscape painting*, Octopus Books, London, 1981

English, P. W. and Mayfield, R.C. (eds), *Man, space, and environment*, Oxford University Press, New York, 1972

Fisher, J. (ed), *Perceiving artworks*, Temple University Press, Philadelphia, 1980

Gombrich, E. H., *The image and the eye*, Cornell University Press, Ithaca, 1982

Gombrich, E. H., Hochberg, J., and Black, M., *Art, perception and reality*, John Hopkins University Press, Baltimore, 1972

Meinig, D. W. (ed), *The interpretation of ordinary landscapes*, New York, Oxford University Press, 1979

Moore, G. T. and Golledge R.G., *Environmental knowing*, Davden, Hutchinson and Ross, Stroudsburg, 1979

Powell, J. M., *Mirrors of the new world*, Australian National University Press, Canberra, 1978

Rapoport, A., *Australia as human setting*, Angus and Robertson, Sydney, 1972

Smith, B., *The spectre of Truganini*, Australian Broadcasting Commission, 1981

Smith, B., *Place, taste and tradition*, Oxford University Press, Melbourne, 1979

Splatt, W. and Bruce, S., *100 masterpieces of Australian landscape painting*, Rigby, Adelaide, 1978